CONCERTOS

NO COLLECTIVE

EMERGENCY PLAYSCRIPTS
UGLY DUCKLING PRESSE
BROOKLYN, NEW YORK

CONCERTOS
COPYRIGHT NO COLLECTIVE, 2011

EMERGENCY PLAYSCRIPTS #2

SERIES EDITOR
YELENA GLUZMAN

SERIES PUBLISHERS
THE BROS. LUMIÈRE

ISBN 978-1-933254-75-3

FIRST EDITION, 2011
UGLY DUCKLING PRESSE
232 THIRD STREET, E002
BROOKLYN, NY 11215
>WWW.UGLYDUCKLINGPRESSE.ORG<

DISTRIBUTED BY
SMALL PRESS DISTRIBUTION
1341 SEVENTH STREET
BERKELEY, CA 94710
>WWW.SPDBOOKS.ORG<

PRINTED IN THE USA

CONCERTOS

No Collective

CONCERTOS

A: You're reading a playscript which describes and prescribes the writing process and performance of *CONCERTOS*, first written between June 10 and August 14, 2008, by You Nakai and premiered by No Collective on August 14 of the same year in Tokyo... and written once again approximately two years later, this time in language, that is to say in English, in the form of a playscript, between February 22 and June 10, 2010, in New York, Kraków, Wien, Nesebar, Ravda, Alexandroupolis, and Samothraki.

B: The dramatis personae of *CONCERTOS* will be four performers, one or several dogs, one or several birds, and several undetermined, unknown performers.

C: This script assembles descriptions of past and prescriptions for future... both tempor... temporalities set in relation to any given present in which *CONCERTOS* is written, read, or performed... again.

D: You just read that No Collective performed at the premier. They consisted of Yuko Asaoka, Midori Kubota, You Nakai, Hikaru Toho, Moe the Shiba-dog, Flip the Pigeon, and several still unidentified performers.

A: You're finding performers specified as A, B, C, D, and assigning your own names to each letter.

You're also giving specific values for every asterisk indicating variables.

B: ACT ONE, SCENE ONE... The play will now start with the four performers coming together for a music performance...

C: Having performers who can play any specific instrument is nice but not a requisite for everybody. Professional ones tend to quit easily anyway... fools, statistically speaking. So two instrumentalists out of four. That's good.

D: Then we briefly explained what instruments were used in 2008.

A: Right... so say you're playing Asaoka, D, then you're using two cheap keyboards and many many amplified objects.

B: There'll be a camera, a fan, some bread, knife and cutting board, a kettle on a stove, tuning whistle…

C: If you play the other characters… Midori plays a grand piano. You plays an acoustic guitar with contact microphones. And effects units. Hikaru plays a double bass. And several percussive instruments. Everyone plays a dog whistle, birdcall. And hums.

D: You whistled:

A: ********

B: But readers will choose any instrument, though dog whistles and birdcalls must be kept.

C: ACT ONE, SCENE TWO. Here, you read the numbered pages of this script aloud from the first to the last. Speed and inclusion of silences are unspecified, but you spend the same time on each page. You record this reading on a sequencer.

D: So you rehearsed… about a page per minute.

A: Okay, setting up the sequencer now… and the volume… testing… yeah, that's fine… everybody on page one? Ready… go…

B: When we're done, we will go out for a drink. Then I will ask all you… you all three questions. What's the music that you've heard most in your life, that you like the most, and that you hate most?

C: *********, *************, ***********.

D: I wrote my answers on a piece of paper, thinking how stupid these questions were, especially the second one. Did we change our answers if they overlapped?

A: Yeah, D... a list of twelve pieces of music is what we're making.

B: My answers will be added here too. And may curses be bestowed upon those who complain. When everybody finishes, all the recordings of the music listed will be collected.

C: Hey... the number of asterisks doesn't match my letters.

D: So then I said... C, I forgot to say this, but the asterisks didn't have to correspond to the number of letters.

A: You're now creating a mix track on the sequencer using the collected recordings.

B: We'll use the same sequencer we recorded our reading with.

C: Look here... see this recording of our reading? First, split this track in half...

yeah, right at the middle... okay, we only use this first half for now... any shift between the reader, like every time you stop and I start... or the occurrence of any chosen word... like *this*, let's say... are read as structural markers for laying out these fragments of collected music... yeah, use this other track beneath.

D: I said *this*, twice...

A: But everything is being included, D... every word the others say... so *this* is occurring for the twelfth time now... if *this* is the chosen word, then *this* is going to be the fourteenth marker.

B: We'll take sound cues from our reading to switch from any fragment of the collected music to another, then overlay the second half of the reading on this mix.

C: Exactly...

D: **************

A: These asterisks are being written here for D, B and C to fill them out in any way they want, making a small intervention to the structural markings.

B: *

C: **********

****

D: ACT ONE, SCENE THREE... A handed us graphic notation scores, one for each, these ones reprinted in the following pages, saying they were to be used with the *pre-text*, the two-layered track composed of the mix of the collected music and the second half of our reading, to determine the parametric constraints within which the *pre-text* was to be read.

A: Yeah, like D just said, you're getting one score each, everybody. Doesn't matter which. You're using them with the *pre-text*. Each of these squares is representing a time bracket. And these signs inside are instructing the six sound parameters that you're using within that bracket.

B: C'll ask...

C: What sound parameters?

D: You replied:

A: Yeah, well I'm explaining the time brackets first, everybody, we're reading these colors as bracket types,

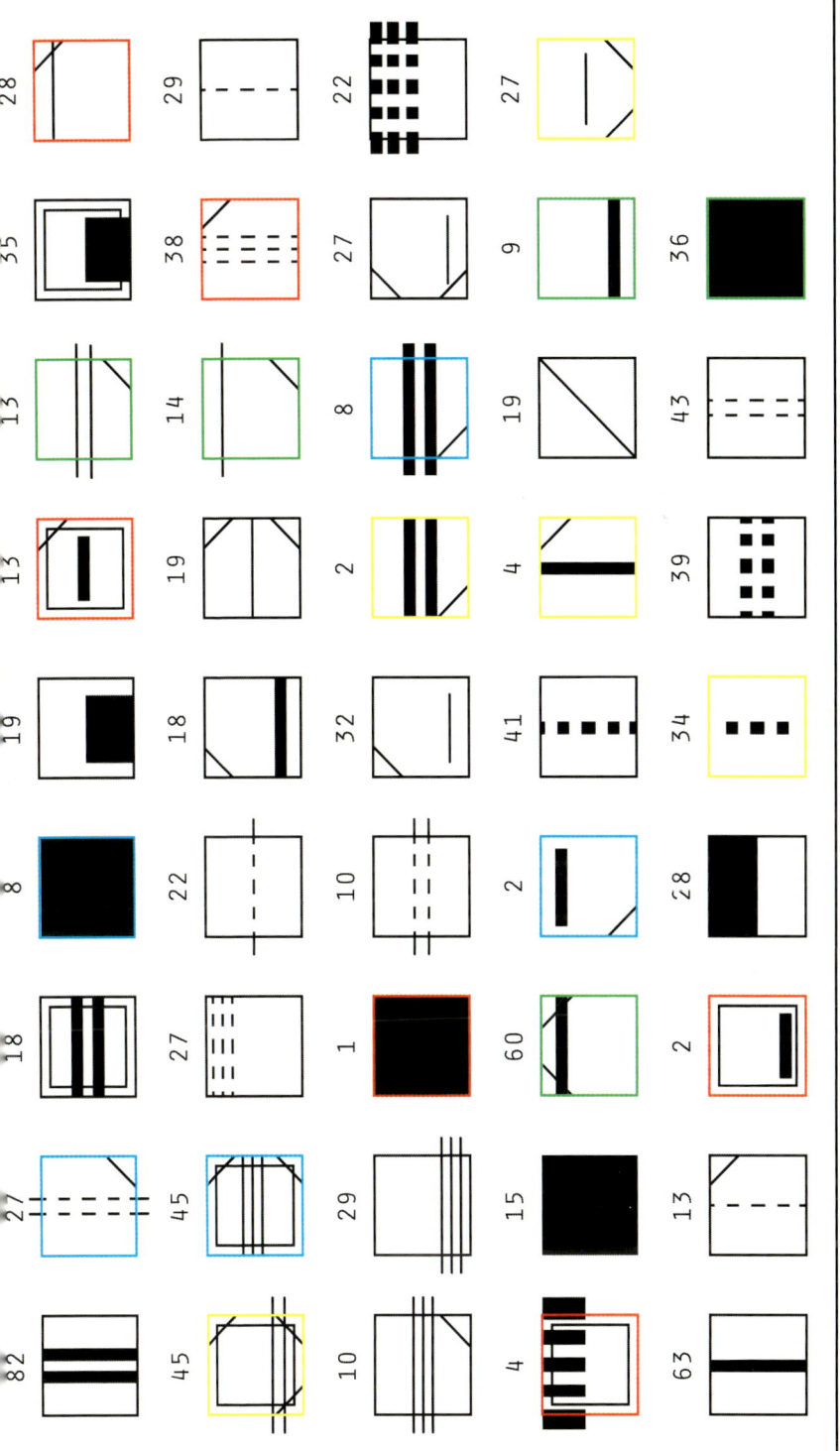

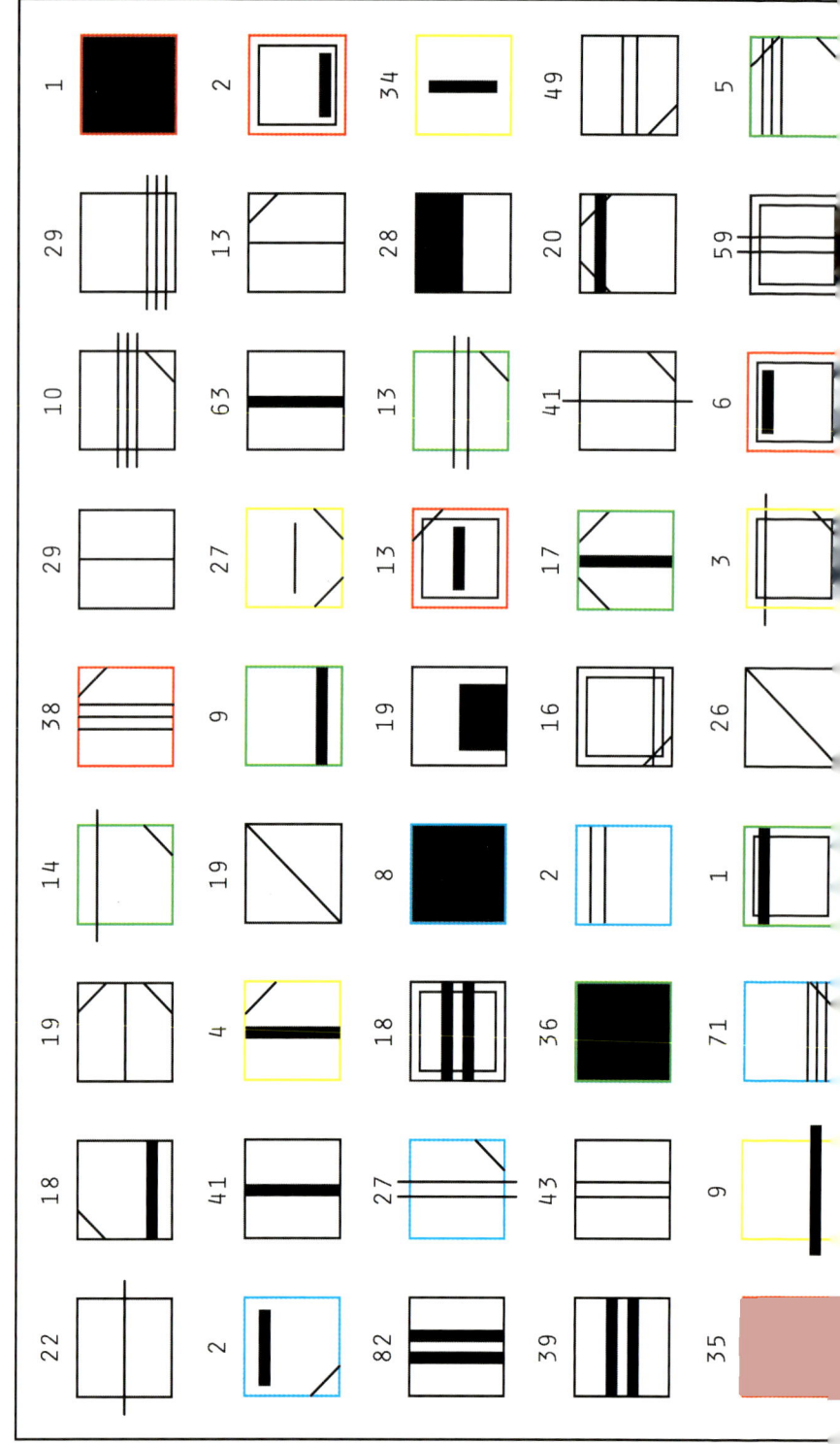

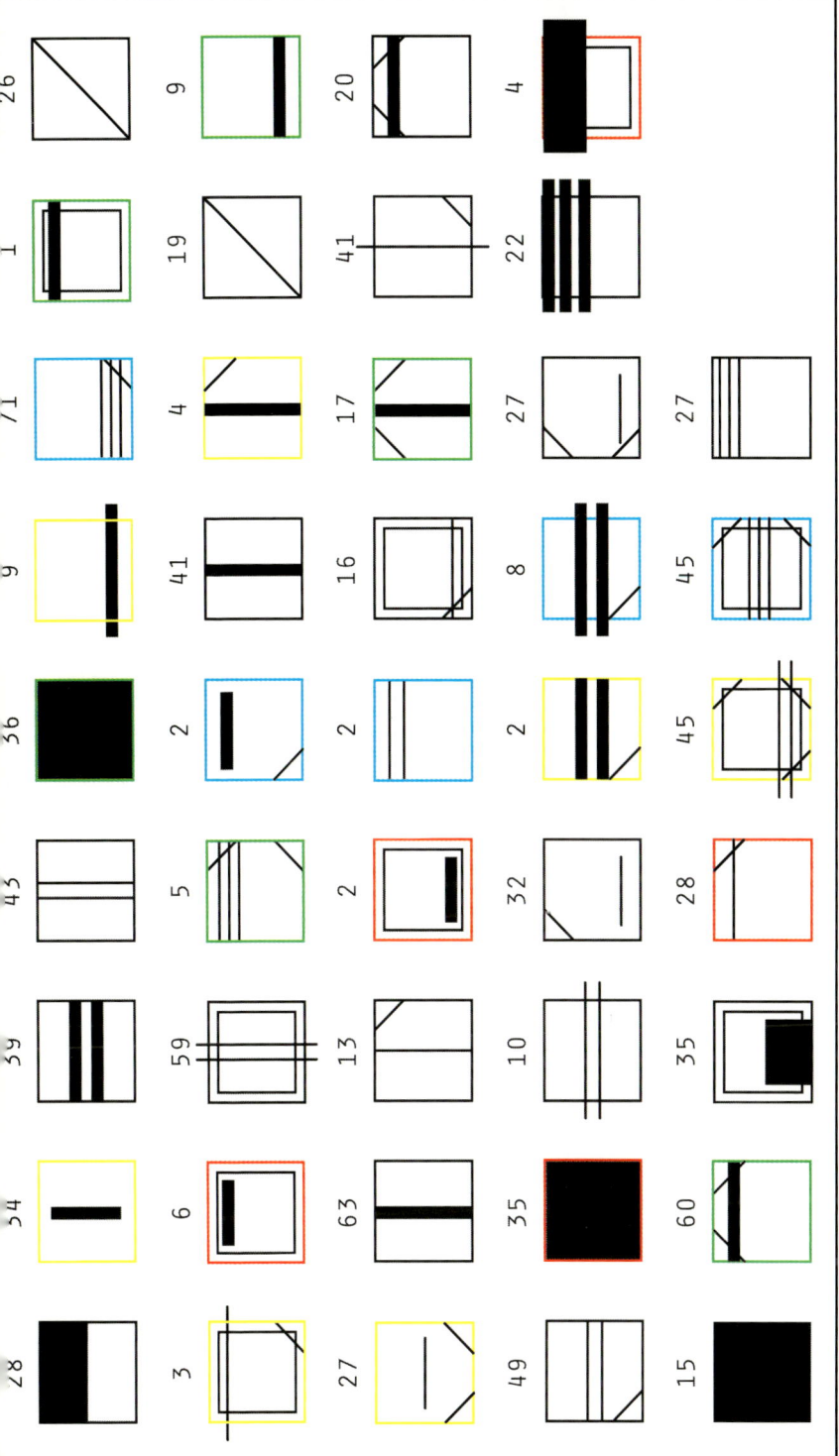

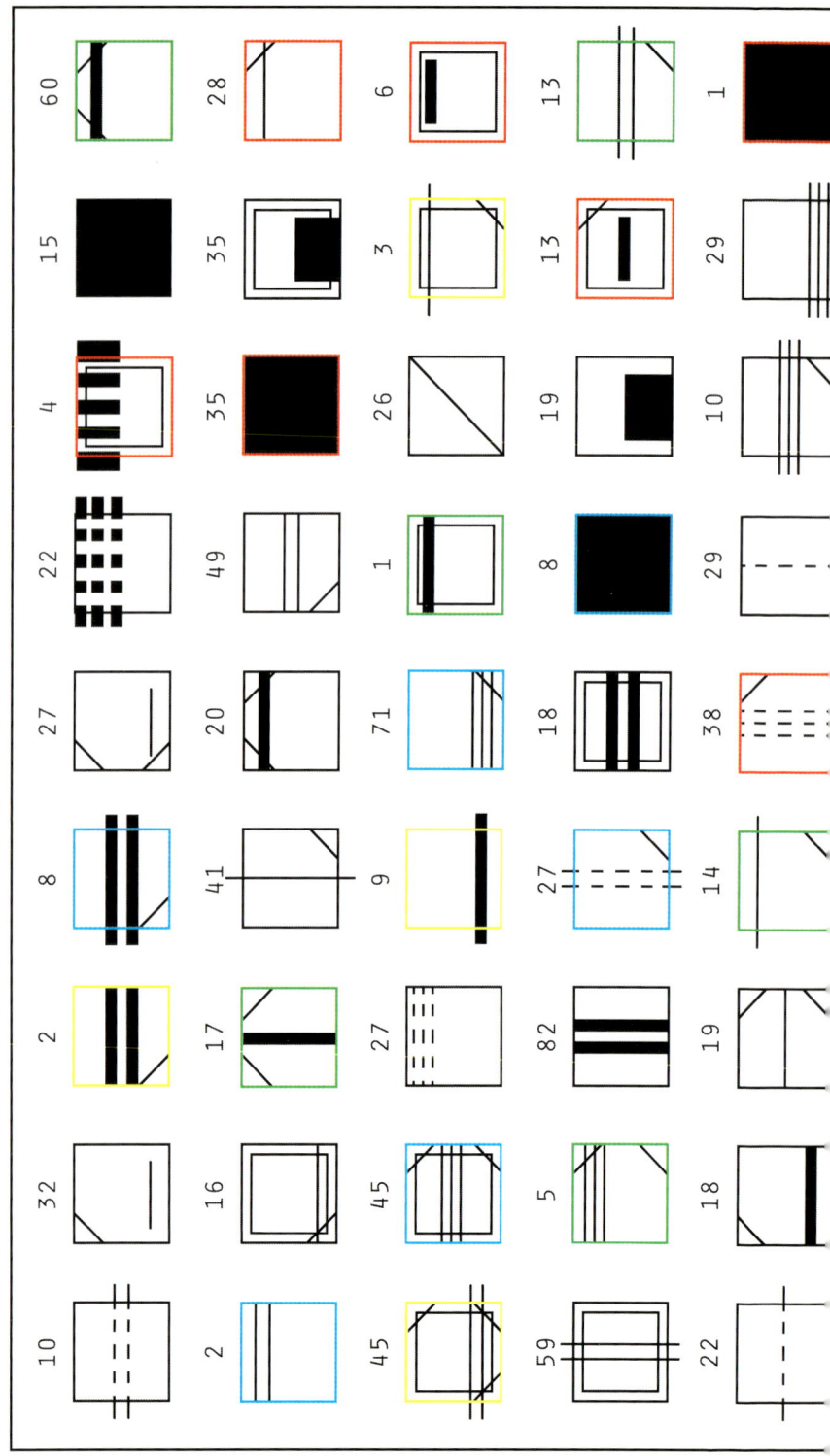

the different ways to articulate the *pre-text*... red is instructing change of music; blue, any chosen sound cue; green, change of the narrating performer; yellow, any chosen word cue.

B: What's listened to in the *pre-text* will either be the mix or the reading track. But never both simultaneously. People say ears don't have lids, unlike eyes. But ears will open and close selectively, unlike eyes which seem incapable of selection.

C: But what about the black brackets... ?

D: Yeah, B forgot that one. Black was free to choose whichever articulation, or to combine several.

A: I am explaining now that these numbers above the brackets determine the length of each bracket by indicating how many changes or cues are to be read.

B: C will explain further...

C: Okay, so for cues,

you pick any type of sound, words, sound aggregates, or silence, and count the number of its occurrence or duration... start from the top left of the score and proceed, bracket by bracket, towards right... so if your number is 59 and your cue, words, counting the leng... the number of words gives you the bracket length.

D: The parameters were... *instrument* or type of sound source, *register, articulation, horizontal density, vertical density* and *intensity.*

A: *Instrument* is being instructed by the number of frames, a blackened bracket, or a slash across the bracket. B's having that next.

B: *******************.

C: As we follow the score...

D: But in the performance,

a singular frame meant one instrument or sound source including vocals, doubled frame meant simultaneous use of multiple instruments or sound sources, blackened bracket was no instrument or do not play, and slashed bracket meant non-instrument.

A: If I have non-instrument, I'm performing any action without intentional musical sound production... so I am talking now...

B: And perhaps someone will reply like this... or question...

C: ...any action?

D: Any action described by coupling a verb and a noun, so like: A explained *register*... after I read this line...

A: Performers are dividing their instrument's pitch domain into three parts: high, middle, low... otherwise distributing them among several instruments.

B: The vertical position of lines will denote high, middle, low accordingly, or if the lines are vertical, it'll be free: to select any or combine all.

C: *Articulation* can be discrete: inserting gaps between consecutive events. This is for dashed lines. Continuous: avoiding gaps. That's with straight lines. Or free: choosing either or combining both. When there's a diagonal line on the lower left corner of the bracket.

D: You read *horizontal density*, the number of sounds compared to sounds in the *pre-text*, from a line's length in relation to the bracket frame, which was shorter, equal, or longer, corresponding to less, same or more sounds, or otherwise a diagonal line on the upper right corner indicated free.

A: Although nobody is mentioning them, these parameters are being illustrated here for your reference.

B: *Vertical density*, the number of sounds played simultaneously, will be indicated by the number of lines… a single line: a singular sound… double lines: aggregate, or two to three sounds… triple lines: cluster, or more than three sounds… diagonal line on the upper left corner: free… and if the instrument can only play one note at a time, several instruments will be used.

C: Line width indicates *intensity*…

D: The wider, the stronger. Weak, neutral, or strong. A diagonal line on the lower right corner meant free. But hey… could you all hear your instruments? If not, *intensity* was the degree of implemented force.

A: We're reading from these scores, the parametric constraints within which we're each creating our musical reactions to the *pre-text*. We're simultaneously playing these individual responses while listening to the *pre-text* on headphones. That constitutes Movement One of *CONCERTOS*.

B: *CONCERTOS* will have three movements, following the tradition. All of the same length.

C: *******************.

D: You mentioned how long, C, but that varied for each performance... according to how fast you read this script, which determined the duration of the first movement... and so consequently, the other two as well...

A: Performers are putting their individually constructed parts together now, making sounds in studios, etcetera, here in ACT ONE, SCENE FOUR, which is going to last at least a month.

B: They'll rehearse.

C: Okay, here's a headphone distributor... and headphones for each.

D: Only the rehearsal of Movement One was explained in this part of the script, and Movement Two and Three were explained and thus performed later, as other scenes.

A: Connecting a player with the *pre-text* to the headphone distributor...

B: Everything you play will be amplified using any speakers, but no P.A., and volume will be adjusted between the speakers as equally balanced as possible... while you'll all have headphones on from which the *pre-text* will be played, meaning that only the assembly of individual responses to the *pre-text* will be heard outside the headphones, meaning that you will have to record every time you rehearse through the movement since no one will be able to hear the result in real time...

C: ACT ONE, SCENE FIVE. Sometime during SCENE FOUR, make flyers. Three versions of different sizes, design, different titles in different languages, instructing the same time and place.

D: Uh... the three titles, you were saying in this scene, A, should each reflect the multiple aspects of this work in different ways... in 2008 they were,

CONCERTO NO. 1, umm, how did you pronounce this, *ALIAJ CIRKVITOJ*? and *SI ME NON VIDEAS, ESSE NEGABIS AVEM*, right?

A: Whatever, now I am making 300 copies of each flyer, all numbered, and inserting them secretly in freezines and/or magazines adequate to each design, in book and record stores.

B: You'll put a notice about free tickets on every flyer. It'll instruct a specific place, maybe a store, where the visitor can be given a closed envelope.

C: Inside each envelope, title of a book and map for a used bookstore, different for each... inside this bookstore, the book, inside the book, the free ticket, with the following instructions: "To enter free: 1. Show this ticket when entering the venue. 2. Follow the given instructions as accurately as possible. 3. Do not show or talk about this instruction to anybody else."

D: So we basically instructed them to go to a bookstore and sneak out the tickets from these books... right, but how many envelopes were there? I thought there were about five different instructions... or six? and... three copies of each? umm... do you remember, A?

A: ?

B: Well, D and A, that's okay, you'll recall as we go writing the instructions down, I'm sure...

C: Five instructions. Three copies. Fifteen envelopes. Here are the notes, so just read.

D: "Waited for the quietest moment in the whole performance and made the loudest sound possible. If after accomplishing this, a quieter moment occurred, I repeated the instruction."

A: You're now reading the second instruction: "Bring a headphone and wear it for at least half of the performance. If you find any other person following the same instruction, shout to him/her:

B: '********!'"

C: Oh, B…

D: "If anyone started clapping, I asked him/her, be quiet…

A: You're raising your voice higher every time you say this."

B: That's three, so there will be two more now… the longer ones about animals… but will they fit here?

C: You bet.

D: "When you heard somebody shout, 'turn the lights up!!' you went after the bird, trying to catch it, and if you succeeded, put the bird in the birdcage shouting, 'this is animal cruelty!' then took off the attached contact microphone and put it onto yourself, but you gave up if you couldn't accomplish this before the lights dimmed, and if you noticed any other person following the same instruction, you cooperated."

A: ...You're next.

B: "When someone goes after the bird, you'll try to catch the dog, shouting:

C: 'This is animal cruelty! I'm taking these speakers off this poor animal and putting them on myself!

D: ...Help!'

A: You're cooperating with people following the same instruction...

B: You'll give up if you can't accomplish this instruction before the lighting dims."

C: Make these free tickets with one instruction in each, sneak them into books in the following bookstores:

D: ****, ****, *****, ****, *****, ****.

A: Follow me as I'm going to search for a place to handout envelopes... preferably a store of a friend... I'm doing this performance, is it okay if...

B: This will probably be around the middle of the script… so the recording of the reading will be split around here, if not a bit before or after…

C: ACT ONE, SCENE SIX, where Movement Two and Three are rehearsed for about two weeks, for which the recording of Movement One is used, as the *pre-text* for Movement Two, and the same scores are used again with changes concerning bracket types.

D: Weren't scores… bigger?

A: We're no longer using auditory cues in this scene. Instead, we're using visual or task-based cues. We're redefining these time brackets accordingly.

B: The red brackets will indicate visual cues from audiences. Like, umm, eye contact between performer and audience, or between audiences. Or, whenever a person passes a specific point in space. That kind of thing.

C: Bracket numbers assign the number of cue event occurrence. Blue brackets also indicate visual cues but from animals, not humans.

D: Hey... weren't these scores bigger originally?

A: ...Performers are enlarging them...

B: For the green brackets... you will derive temporal units from the physical properties of your body or instrument. Like the length of your breath... one full bow stroke... time it takes to boil a kettle... size of your hand...

C: If yellow, execute a mental task, like recalling what you had for previous meals, names of relatives, etcetera, this... using bracket numbers to determine necessary boundaries for each task. Still consider black as free. Increase, from Movement One, the rate of non-musical sound production or activities other than playing instruments.

D: You were all free to move around and encouraged to switch instruments, so you were talking with your audience, A, and

C, you were getting a drink, B went to the bathroom, sort of a prolonged intermission, still following the score, performing in reaction to the *pre-text*, but in this scene you now recited the list of equipment used:

A: *, *, **, *, **, *, *, *, **, **, *.

B: You will assign the names of the actual equipment in those asterisks. They will be: Three mp3/wav recorders to record and playback each movement. A headphone distributor to distribute the played-back *pre-text*. Long extension cords to connect each performer's headphones to the distributor.

C: There's more, everybody… small mixers for each. Four tracks would be enough. Speakers for each. Two wearable microphones attached to two sets of wireless transceivers. Matrix switcher with at least four inputs and four outputs.

D: We haven't mentioned cell phones.

A: I'm further adding to the list, a tiny microphone for the bird(s) and a small speaker with wheels for the dog(s), each connected to a set of wireless transceivers, a cord to connect each cell phone to each mixer… each performer's phone number is printed on every flyer, along with instructions that if they're arriving late, they must call:

B: *********, *********, *********, *********.

C: And when they do, you amplify them via mixers. Also in Movement Three, you go outside the venue and call the performer at the venue. And play the street sounds from the speakers.

D: You connected each instrument and telephone into each mixer, and from there to each speaker, while A's mixer output, two sets of receivers from portable microphones, and the receiver from the bird's microphone were connected to the matrix switcher, outputting to all the speakers plus the transmitter to the dog's amplifier…

except for the animal circuit, the matrix switcher wasn't used until Movement Three, in which the two recorders recording the previous movements were connected to A's mixer, and played out simultaneously.

A: ACT ONE,

B: SCENE SEVEN.

C: Let's go out to find a bird and a dog.

D: Two years ago, You rented a dog, Moe, from a rental pet shop, and caught a pigeon, Flip, with a net, which took You two whole days.

A: For a couple of days… Flip is staying in, in a birdcage. Moe is running around. They're being taken care of. Joining rehearsals. A tiny microphone is being attached to Flip's leg. A small speaker with wheels is attached to Moe's collar.

B: ACT TWO, SCENE ONE. This act will be performed on a single day. First, we'll set up?

C: You bet…

D: There was no stage, everybody, you dispersed... locating a spot where one other performer became out of sight.

A: No chairs for audience...

B: Lighting will be medium level, animals will be set loose, we'll go out... ACT TWO, SCENE TWO.

C: Ask everyone which piece they came to see...

D: ********?

A: ******************.

B: They'll reply something like that, then line up in one of three spots around the venue according to their answers... from lines A and C, only line B will be visible, from line B, both A and C will be visible.

C: D, ask the questions and charge the tickets. A, line up in spot A. B, to line B. Me, line C. Remember the people in your line.

D: It was time... everybody in line A, you entered first... two minutes later, line B... from anoth... another two, then C...

A: ACT TWO, SCENE THREE... D, you're entering with C.

B: A will merge with the audience until I enter... now start to set up, A, I'll wait for C's entry.

C: These lines proceed here... but we actually never speak nor look at each other. Nor at the audience. We put headphones on.

D: Hey, everybody connected their cell phones to the mixers for the latecomers...

okay?

A: Movement One is starting now. Someone is pressing the play button for the *pre-text* and the record button for two mp3/wav recorders at the same time... now.

B: ACT TWO, SCENE FOUR, when Movement One is over, you'll switch the mp3/wav player containing the *pre-text* with one of the two recorders that recorded Movement One. You'll press play for this new *pre-text*, simultaneously with record on a newly set mp3/wav recorder, yelling then to any venue staff:

C: ...Turn the lights up!

D: You followed the score/*pre-text* and moved around, creating a web of extension cords.

A: In opposition to Movement One, where all eye contact and communication were averted, performers are now taking most cues from eye contact with each other, and engaging in communication as part of this performance...

and when a cue refers to the audience, each performer is only taking into account those who he/she lined up with outside the venue, ignoring all the other people.

B: This script won't specify who... but anyone of you playing Asaoka, will try to catch that bird. The score and *pre-text* will be followed. If someone criticizes about animal cruelty, your reply will simply be:

C: ***************!

D: Movement Two ended. The bird was caught, put back into the birdcage. Performers took headphones off, leaving a web of entangled cords.

A: ACT TWO, SCENE FIVE. D is leaving the venue now, carrying the bir... birdcage.

B: Will you turn the lights off before exiting, D...

C: In this scene, D exits, leaving the venue in a total darkness, while A connects the two recorders... recorders with recordings of previous two movements to his/her mixer, and B and I each put on portable microphones connected to transmitters… A then connects the output from the mixer and the two receivers paired with B and my transmitter to the matrix switcher.

D: Outside… I released the bird at a safe place, then called A's cell phone as I strolled around.

A: Hello? D?

B: For the input to the matrix switcher, we'll have the two recordings of past movements, the real-time transmission of street sounds and the two receivers paired with portable microphones, and for the output, four speakers of each performer and the dog amplifier, that'll be labeled A to E accordingly, and now we'll move around the space, through the web of extension cords, while A plays out the two recordings in sync.

C: Follow this same score again, A… counting silently each bracket number gives the bracket length... the number of lines inside each bracket gives the number of speakers... and the bracket color gives the speaker combination.

D: So A was looking at the first bracket in his/her score, counting silently to 82 while selecting two speakers.

A: For one/two speakers, black is including speaker A... blue, speaker B... red, speaker C... green, speaker D... yellow, speaker E... for more speakers, black is excluding A... etcetera.

B: ...Ahhhhhhh!!

C: The microphone-performers also count memorized bracket numbers, while staying away from feedback, and make the loudest sound using whatever means at each bracket change, like B just did.

D: Keeping track of time, Asaoka returned to venue at the end of this movement.

A: B/C are gradually increasing their counting speed, using more clapping… D's entry is creating a giant feedback with his/her phone. D's turning on the lights. I'm going to the piano, playing a cadence: C-G7-C.

B: *************************

C: You don't have to clap anymore B, it's the audience's turn to take over the clapping…

You should instead bow, thank the secret guest performers, etcetera. Then, after packing all the equipments, drinking, lamenting everything that went wrong, you have an INTERMISSION of eighteen months.

D: ACT THREE, SCENE ONE. Approximately a year and half after the first performance. A publisher asked me, or I asked a publisher, to publish the description and prescription of *CONCERTOS* in the form of a playscript.

A: Which is what you're reading now... So you're rewriting this playscript and publishing it under your own name. You're replacing all proper nouns, dates and numbers. You're excluding, that is, everything about previous versions of *CONCERTOS* and its authors.

B: Who'll write this?

C: Well B, one of us, or all of us together, but more important is how we write it, that other than the necessary replacements of names and dates, we make no deliberate omissions, transformations of any part of this script... we also keep the title.

D: After all the necessary re... revisions were made, the script was read aloud and recorded. The structure of the book was derived from this reading, a page per minute.

A: To bind the book, you're using 60 pages minimum. You're putting whatever was read in a minute onto one page, leaving any remaining pages blank, unnumbered. You're scripting accurately all the inevitable pronunciations and/or accidental reiterations in the reading preserved in the recording.

B: How... fast will this be read?

C: I don't care about the speed. All I care is that I finish writing this exactly two years after the commencement of the first writing. June 10.

D: ACT THREE, SCENE TWO. We published this from the publisher:

A: **************************************.

B: As you excluded the past of this work from this script, you'll now exclude yourself from its future by abandoning contact with any of the subsequent publications and performances of this work once this script is published, performing it as your work whenever you want, but letting *CONCERTOS* itself extend a life and time of its own beyond you.

D: A work, after all, was a construct enabling the reenactment of a radical shift of thought and/or sensation, but to make iteration possible, it had to close itself somewhere.

B: So ours will end here.

D: *

CONCERTOS BY No COLLECTIVE

Nine hundred copies of this first edition were printed and bound in the spring of 2011 by MCNAUGHTON & GUNN in the state of Michigan, near the Saline River, using 100% recycled, FSC-certified paper. The covers were printed offset on Fabriano Tiziano paper by POLYPRINT DESIGN on the shores of the Hudson River in New York City, and letterpressed at the UGLY DUCKLING PRESS workshop on the Gowanus Canal in Brooklyn, New York. Design by DON'T LOOK NOW! with assistance from Emily Rabkin. Typeset in Akzidenz Gothic and Orator typefaces.

EMERGENCY PLAYSCRIPTS promotes texts which, through their performance, can expand the practice of theater. The series is edited by Yelena Gluzman and published by Auguste & Louis Lumière exclusively for UGLY DUCKLING PRESSE.

EMERGENCY PLAYSCRIPTS:

HELLO FAILURE BY KRISTEN KOSMAS
(2009)

CONCERTOS BY NO COLLECTIVE
(2011)

NOT KNOWING BY MIKE TAYLOR
(FORTHCOMING 2012)